Famous Explorers

La Salle

Jeff
Donaldson-Forbes

The Rosen Publishing Group's
PowerKids Press™
New York

To Marcus Octaviano and Steven Octaviano Jr.

Published in 2002 by The Rosen Publishing Group, Inc.
29 East 21st Street, New York, NY 10010

Photo Credits: pp. 4, 8, 9, 11 (left), 11 (right), 12 (bottom), 14, 15, 16 (left), 16 (right), 19, 20 (right) © North Wind Pictures; p. 7 © Newberry Library, Chicago/SuperStock; 12 (top) illustration by Maria Melendez; p. 13 © CORBIS/Bettmann; p. 20 (left) © The Granger Collection.

First Edition

Book Design: Maria E. Melendez and Felicity Erwin

Project Editor: Kathy Campbell

Donaldson-Forbes, Jeff.
   La Salle / Jeff Donaldson-Forbes
      p. cm. — (Famous explorers)
Includes index.
ISBN 0-8239-5830-2 (lib. bdg.)
1. La Salle, Robert Cavelier, sieur de, 1643–1687—Juvenile literature. 2. Explorers—North America—Biography—Juvenile literature. 3. Explorers—France—Biography—Juvenile literature. 4. Canada—Discovery and exploration—French—Juvenile literature. 5. Canada—History—To 1763 (New France)—Juvenile literature. 6. Mississippi River Valley—Discovery and exploration—French—Juvenile literature. 7. Mississippi River Valley—History—To 1803—Juvenile literature. [1. La Salle, Robert Cavelier, sieur de, 1643–1687. 2. Explorers. 3. Mississippi River—Discovery and exploration.] I. Title. II. Series.
   F1030.5 .D66 2002
   977'.01'092—dc21

00-011108

Manufactured in the United States of America

Contents

4

A Good Student

René-Robert Cavelier was born in 1643, in the city of Rouen, France. His father, Jean, was a merchant. Jean was in the business of buying and selling goods. He provided his family with the finest comforts in life.

By the time he was nine years old, René-Robert attended a school taught by **Jesuits**. Jesuits are priests who belong to a religious order in the Catholic Church. The Jesuits are known for their work as **missionaries** and teachers. At the age of 15, René-Robert moved to Paris to begin training as a Jesuit priest. René-Robert was a very good student. He studied **astronomy**, **geography**, and **navigation**. He wanted to travel rather than to become a priest. He left the Jesuit school. In 1666, he sailed on a ship to New France. New France was a royal **province** of France. It was located in North America, in the eastern part of today's Canada.

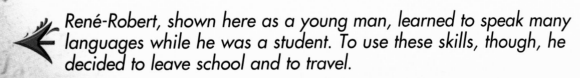

René-Robert, shown here as a young man, learned to speak many languages while he was a student. To use these skills, though, he decided to leave school and to travel.

A New Life, a New Name

In 1663, King Louis XIV **declared** New France a royal province. The king sent an army and thousands of French people to settle the area. People living in New France were missionaries, farmers, fur traders, and **explorers**. René-Robert's older brother, Jean, was a priest living in the town of Montreal. The Catholic Church owned land near Montreal. The land was perfect for fur trading. It was also open to attacks by Native Americans. The Catholic Church granted René-Robert a large piece of land outside Montreal. In return, he agreed to invite other French settlers to join him.

René-Robert wanted to **impress** his friends in New France. He began using the title Sieur de la Salle, which means Lord of La Salle. La Salle was the name of an estate that René-Robert's family owned in France. Soon René-Robert became known only as La Salle.

This map of New France shows how the people of La Salle's time thought North America looked. French explorer Louis Jolliet, who knew La Salle, drew this map in 1673–74. Almost all the land was covered by forests.

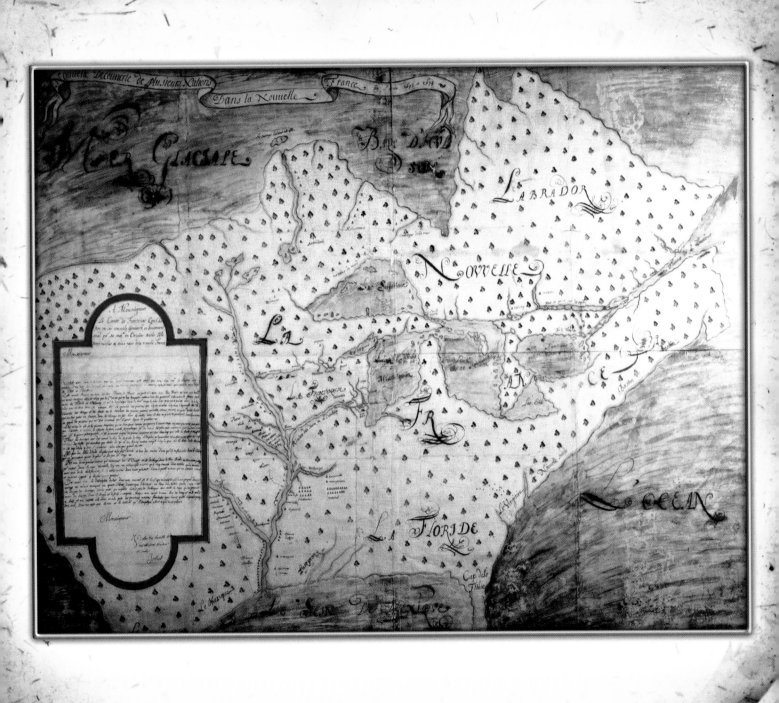

8

Meeting the Native Americans

La Salle built a house on his new land in New France in 1667. There he met Native Americans who lived in the woods nearby. La Salle's skill with languages helped him speak with them. La Salle began fur trading with them. Two groups of Native Americans lived near La Salle in New France. The first group was the Algonquins. The Algonquins were **allies** of the French. The second group, the Iroquois, was an enemy of the Algonquins and the French. The Iroquois was made up of five Native American nations, including the Senecas, who joined together to fight against their enemies. Shortly before La Salle arrived in New France, the Iroquois agreed to make peace with the French settlers.

 Left: Algonquins are shown here building lodges, or huts. Above: An Iroquois warrior uses a bow and arrow. The bow and arrow were used to hunt and to fight enemies.

Two Rivers

During the winter of 1668, La Salle let some Iroquois stay on his land. They told him about two rivers called the Ohio and the Mississippi. They also told him that the rivers flowed to the sea. La Salle was excited by this story. He believed the rivers might flow all the way to the Pacific Ocean. At that time many explorers believed there was a **waterway**, called the Northwest Passage, which connected the Atlantic Ocean and the Pacific Ocean. They looked for this waterway because it would give them a fast route to China where they could trade furs for spices and silk.

The Iroquois agreed to lead La Salle to the great rivers. He had to raise money for an **expedition**. The Catholic Church asked him to join two missionaries who were going to travel along the Mississippi to **convert** the Native Americans to **Christianity**.

Top: A missionary tries to convert a group of Native Americans. La Salle had to join two missionaries whose trip down the Ohio had already been planned. Bottom: A French map of 1697 shows the Mississippi (Messchasipi) River and the Ohio (Hohio) River. La Salle hoped to sail down these rivers.

Ohio River

Mississippi River

Saint Lawrence River

LAKE
HURON

MONTREAL

SAULT SAINTE MARIE

La Salle ?

LAKE
ONTARIO

ATLANTIC
OCEAN

LAKE ERIE

This map shows the route La Salle's expedition supposedly took when it tried to find the Ohio River. The expedition split into two groups. One half went farther west and up to Sault Sainte Marie. No one is sure about where La Salle's half of the expedition headed. Most people believe it returned to Montreal.

The First Expedition

In July 1669, La Salle traveled with the two missionaries, the Iroquois guides, and 20 other men. They sailed in canoes from the Saint Lawrence River, at Montreal, to Lake Ontario. After they crossed Lake Ontario, they visited an Iroquois nation called the Senecas. During the visit, the explorers saw something horrible. The Senecas captured a warrior from a different Native American group. They tortured and killed him. La Salle and his men grew afraid for their own safety. Then their Iroquois guides refused to help them any longer. The expedition split into two groups. The missionaries traveled west toward Lake Erie, where they believed there were friendly Native Americans. The second group, La Salle's, supposedly headed back to Montreal.

 La Salle and some of the members of his expedition sail down a waterway in a birchbark canoe. Most people who study La Salle's life believe that he never found the Ohio River during his first expedition in 1669.

Starting Over

La Salle's first expedition to find the Ohio River failed, according to most historians. No one is certain what La Salle did during the following two years. Some historians believe that he managed to discover the Ohio River on his own. They base their beliefs on **journals** of La Salle's travels. Most historians, though, think that he spent these two years with Native Americans, studying their lives and speaking their languages.

This picture of Count de Frontenac was copied from an 1890 statue. Frontenac asked La Salle to be in charge of a new fort.

By 1671, La Salle was back in Montreal. He had spent most of his own money on the first expedition and needed to make more money. He met the new governor of New France, Count de Frontenac. The men became friends. Frontenac wanted a new peace

This map shows Fort Frontenac and French and Native American settlements in 1703.

treaty with the Iroquois. This treaty would allow the French to trade with the Iroquois. It also would let them establish a **fort** on the shore of Lake Ontario. La Salle arranged a meeting on July 12, 1673, between Frontenac and the Iroquois. The Iroquois agreed to trade with the French and to let the French build the fort. Frontenac asked La Salle to be in charge of the new fort.

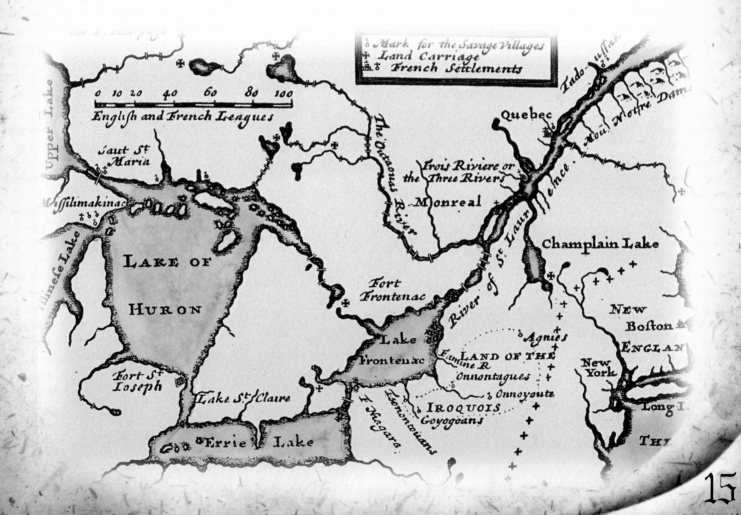

16

The Griffon

La Salle lived at Fort Frontenac for about two years. He became bored with the trading business. In 1674, King Louis XIV of France gave La Salle permission to begin exploring again. To help pay for a new expedition, he built a giant ship on Lake Erie to be used for fur trading. He asked Henry de Tonti, an Italian soldier, to take charge of building the ship, called the *Griffon*. Tonti later became La Salle's second in command and best friend.

The *Griffon* made one voyage on Lake Erie and Lake Huron in August 1679. One month later, La Salle ordered the *Griffon* to return to Fort Frontenac, to cash in its cargo of furs. He wanted to use the money to fund an expedition to explore the Mississippi River. The *Griffon*, though, was never seen again. It might have been destroyed during a storm.

Left: La Salle's ship, the Griffon, built in 1679 on Lake Erie, probably looked a lot like these two ships from the 1683 expedition. Right: In 1677, King Louis XIV of France gave La Salle permission to try to find an outlet leading from the mouth of the Mississippi River to the sea.

The Second Expedition

In 1681–82, La Salle led an expedition to search for the mouth of the Mississippi River. By this time, La Salle believed that the Mississippi emptied into the Gulf of Mexico and not the Pacific Ocean. He wanted to prove that his belief was true. La Salle did not want to build another large ship like the *Griffon*. Instead, his expedition traveled in canoes.

Twenty French explorers and 30 Native Americans traveled with La Salle. In April 1682, the expedition reached the mouth of the Mississippi River near what is today the state of Louisiana. The expedition met many different Native Americans during the journey. La Salle did not care that the Native Americans already thought of the land as their home. Everywhere he traveled, La Salle claimed the land in the name of King Louis XIV of France.

This map shows La Salle's second and third expeditions. In 1682, on his second trip, La Salle sailed down the Mississippi all the way to the Gulf of Mexico. Two years later, on his third expedition, he wanted to find the Mississippi River starting from France and sailing across the Atlantic Ocean.

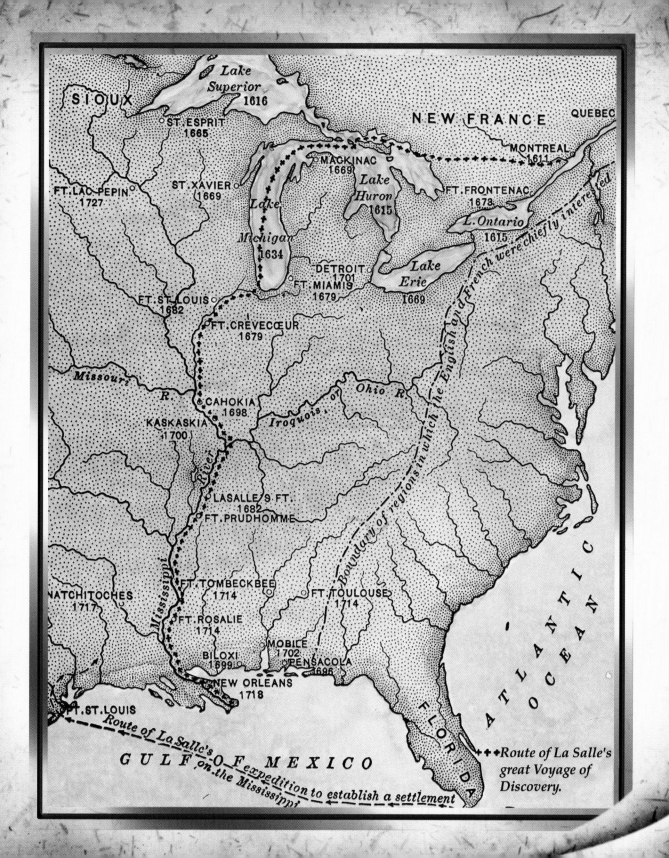

SIOUX

Lake Superior 1616

ST. ESPRIT 1665

NEW FRANCE

QUEBEC

MACKINAC 1669

MONTREAL 1611

FT. LAC-PEPIN 1727

ST. XAVIER 1669

Lake Huron 1615

FT. FRONTENAC 1673

Lake Michigan 1634

L. Ontario 1615

DETROIT 1701

Lake Erie 1669

FT. ST. LOUIS 1682

FT. MIAMIS 1679

FT. CREVECŒUR 1679

Missouri R.

Ohio R.

Iroquois

CAHOKIA 1698

KASKASKIA 1700

River

Boundary of regions in which the English and French were chiefly interested

LASALLE'S FT. 1682

FT. PRUDHOMME

NATCHITOCHES 1717

FT. TOMBECKBEE 1714

FT. TOULOUSE 1714

ATLANTIC OCEAN

FT. ROSALIE 1714

Mississippi

MOBILE 1702

BILOXI 1699

PENSACOLA 1696

NEW ORLEANS 1718

FLORIDA

FT. ST. LOUIS

Route of La Salle's expedition to establish a settlement on the Mississippi

GULF OF MEXICO

++ Route of La Salle's great Voyage of Discovery.

19

La Salle claimed all the lands and waters touched by the Mississippi River for King Louis XIV.

In 1683, La Salle went to France to ask King Louis XIV for money to start a new colony in Louisiana.

The Mouth of the Mississippi

La Salle, Henry de Tonti, and their small crew reached the mouth of the Mississippi River on April 9, 1682. The river flowed into the Gulf of Mexico and La Salle knew he and his crew had reached their goal. La Salle raised the French flag and named the surrounding country after King Louis XIV. He called the new land Louisiana. La Salle claimed all lands that the Mississippi River and its streams touched as French lands. From Canada to Illinois to Louisiana, all these lands became the property of France.

In 1683, La Salle and Tonti established a fort along the Illinois River. They called it Fort St. Louis. Count de Frontenac was no longer the governor of New France. The new governor did not like La Salle and refused to provide any money to support the fort. The governor ordered La Salle to give up the fort.

A Final Voyage

The French king, Louis XIV, supported La Salle's claims in New France and allowed him to take four ships from France to Louisiana. In 1684, La Salle and about 300 people headed for the Gulf of Mexico. La Salle wanted to form a colony at the mouth of the Mississippi. He had not made a map of the mouth of the river when he had first discovered it. The ships sailed past the Mississippi, to Matagorda Bay, on the coast of Texas. The French settlers struggled to live in Texas. In 1687, La Salle and several others set out to find another place for the colony. Some unhappy settlers followed them and killed La Salle. His murder was a sad ending to an amazing life. He always will be remembered as a brave explorer.

La Salle's Timeline

1643 La Salle is born in Rouen, France.

1666 La Salle sets sail for New France in Canada.

1668 Iroquois tell La Salle of two great rivers: the Ohio and the Mississippi.

1669 First expedition goes in search of the Ohio River.

1682 Second expedition finds the mouth of the Mississippi River.

1684 La Salle leaves from France with four ships.

1687 La Salle is killed by angry French settlers.

Glossary

allies (A-lyz) Groups of people that agree to help another group of people.

astronomy (uh-STRA-nuh-mee) The science of the Sun, Moon, planets, and stars.

Christianity (kris–chee-A-nih-tee) A religion based on the teachings of Jesus Christ and the Bible, practiced by Eastern, Roman Catholic, and Protestant groups.

convert (kuhn-VERT) To change religious beliefs.

declared (di-KLAIRD) Announced officially.

expedition (ek-spuh-DIH-shun) A trip for a special purpose, such as scientific study.

explorers (ik-SPLOR-urs) People who travel to different places to learn more about them.

fort (FORT) A strong building or place that can be defended against an enemy.

geography (jee-AH-gruh-fee) The study of Earth's surface, climate, continents, countries, and people.

impress (im-PRES) To have a strong effect on someone's mind or feelings.

Jesuits (JEH-shyoo-wits) Members of a Roman Catholic religious order that is officially called the Society of Jesus.

journals (JER-nuhls) Notebooks in which people write their thoughts.

missionaries (MIH-shuh-nayr-ees) People who teach their religion to people with different beliefs.

navigation (nag-vuh-GAY-shun) A way of figuring out which way a ship is headed.

province (PRAH-vens) One of the main divisions of a country, for example, Canada is divided into provinces rather than states.

treaty (TREE-tee) A formal agreement, especially one between nations, signed and agreed upon by each nation.

waterway (WAH-ter-way) A sea route for ships.

Index

Web Sites

Due to the changing nature of Internet links, PowerKids Press has developed an online list of Web sites related to the subject of this book. This site is updated regularly. Please use this link to access the list: www.powerkidslinks.com/famex/salle/